Liverpool FC

Richard Callaghan
MY FOOTBALL

Designed by **courage**

Text copyright © Richard Callaghan

Design copyright © **courage**

ISBN: 978 1 909486 05 8

First Published 2013

Published in Great Britain by:
My World
Chase House
Rainton Bridge Business Park
Tyne and Wear
DH4 5RA
Tel: 0191 3055165

www.myworld.co.uk

My World is an imprint of Business Education Publishers Ltd.

All rights reserved. No part of this publication, may be reproduced, stored in a retrieval system, or transmitted, in any form or by any means, electronic, mechanical, photocopying, recording or otherwise, without the prior permission of *My World*.

British Cataloguing-in-Publications Data.
A catalogue record for this book is available from the British Library.

Printed in Great Britain by Martins the Printers Ltd.

Liverpool FC

Everton
↓
Everton FC and Athletic Grounds Ltd
↓
Everton Athletic
↓
Liverpool FC

Founding Liverpool

In 1890 there was one football club in Liverpool, Everton. Their home was Anfield, and they were undeniably the city's top team. However, trouble was brewing in the Everton boardroom. After a conflict between the club's committee members and their President and chief creditor, John Houlding, Everton crossed Stanley Park to their new home at Goodison. This left Anfield without a football team, prompting Houlding to found a new side, christened Everton FC and Athletic Grounds Ltd, or Everton Athletic. However, the Football League decreed that there could not be two teams called Everton, and the club's name was changed to Liverpool FC, the club formally established on March 15, 1892.

Friendly Anfield, Liverpool

01/09/1892 / Liverpool vs Rotherham Town

Liverpool /
Ross, Hannah, McLean, Kelso, Que, McBride, Wyllie, Smith, Miller, McVean, Kelvin.

Rotherham Town /
Wharton, Thickett, Turner, Barr, Brown, Rodgers, Longton, Cutts, Leatherbarrow, Pickering, Leather.

Liverpool 7-1 Rotherham Town
(Kelvin, McVean, Wyllie, Wyllie, Miller, Wyllie, Kelvin, Leatherbarrow)

Liverpool's first game saw the thrashing of a Rotherham Town team which had just been crowned Midland League champions for the first time. Liverpool's team was the first in English football to be entirely composed of foreigners, every single member of the new side hailing from north of the border. A Tom Wyllie hat trick, as well as goals from Kelvin and McVean, put Liverpool into a 5-0 lead at the break, with two more goals coming in the second period before the visitors grabbed a consolation strike late on.

BILLY DUNLOP

LEFT BACK

363 GAMES

14 YEARS (1895-1909)

Joining Liverpool in 1895 for £35, William Theodore Dunlop made 363 appearances for the club over 15 years at Anfield, becoming a key member of the 1901 and 1906 title winning teams. An industrious left back, Dunlop may have been known for his ferocity in defence, but he was a man of no little skill, a powerful defender who was vital to that first great Liverpool team. His last appearance came in a 2-2 draw against Bury in 1909. After leaving Liverpool, Dunlop took a job as assistant manager of Sunderland, passing away in 1945.

MANAGERS

Tom Watson
1896-1915

Eyebrows must have been raised in 1896 when 37 year old Tom Watson, with three league championships to his name at Sunderland, left Wearside for Merseyside and the newly promoted Liverpool. Watson's Sunderland had been known as the "Team of All Talents", and he set about replicating their success at his new club. During his time at Anfield he led the club to two league titles, in 1900-01 and 1905-06. Although suffering relegation under his stewardship, he won the Second Division title in 1904-05, and took the club to its first FA Cup Final in 1914. Sadly in 1915 he passed away, aged just 56, the first great manager of Liverpool.

JACK COX

81 GOALS

360 GAMES

12 YEARS (1897-1909)

Born in Liverpool on December 21, 1877, Jack Cox signed for the club from Blackpool during the 1897-98 season for £150, as a financially struggling Blackpool attempted to cut their losses. He became a key part of Tom Watson's side, playing 360 games and contributing 81 goals from left and right wing. Cox was a star of the 1901 and 1906 title winning sides, gaining renown for his pace and trickery on the flanks. In August 1909 he returned to his first club Blackpool to become player-manager, hoping to spearhead a promotion push which unfortunately never materialised, and he retired from football in 1911.

Alex Raisbeck
1898-1909

Arguably Liverpool's first superstar

Arguably Liverpool's first superstar, Polmont born Alex Raisbeck joined Liverpool in 1898 for £350. Just 5 foot 10, Raisbeck was a commanding centre half whose diminutive frame belied his ability to control opposition centre forwards. After missing out on a league and cup double in his first season, Raisbeck captained Watson's team to their two title wins in 1901 and 1906. He left Liverpool in 1909 to return to Scotland, but found himself back at Anfield as a scout following spells as manager of Hamilton Academical, Bristol City, Halifax, Chester and Bath. In all, Alex Raisbeck made 341 appearances for Liverpool, scoring 19 goals.

Stats: Position: Centre Half. Years: 11. Games: 341. Goals: 19.

Anfield

Opened in 1884, Anfield has been home to both of Liverpool's great football clubs. Originally owned by John Orrell, it saw Everton's first league championship in the 1890-91 season, but Everton left the ground in 1892 after a disagreement between John Houlding, then an Everton member, and the other 279 members of the club. Everton left the ground, moving to Goodison Park, and Houlding founded a new football club, Liverpool.

Anfield's first main stand was constructed in 1895 and in 1903 a stand on Anfield Road was built. In 1906, following Liverpool's second league championship, a new stand was built by the famed architect Archibald Leitch on Walton Breck Road. It would go on to become one of the most famous in world football. Named after a famous hill in South Africa where the Lancashire Fusiliers had sustained heavy casualties during the Boer War, the stand was called "Spion Kop" by Liverpool Echo reporter Ernest Edwards. The first ground with a terrace known as a Kop was not Anfield but rather Woolwich Arsenal's Manor Ground, the second stand of which was named the Kop in 1904, two years before Edwards used the name for Anfield's Walton Breck Road stand.

BILL LACEY

29 GOALS

259 GAMES

8 YEARS (1912-1915, 1919-1924)

Irishman Bill Lacey made the trip across Stanley Park from Everton in 1912, beginning what would be a twelve year career at Liverpool. A staggeringly versatile footballer, who appeared in every position on the pitch during his career, Lacey played 259 times for Liverpool, scoring 29 goals. He was in the team which made it to the club's first FA Cup Final in 1914, losing 1-0 to Burnley. Lacey, an international who played for both the Irish and Irish Free State football teams, returned to Ireland during the First World War, guesting for Belfast United and Linfield. He came back to Liverpool in 1919, however, and was an integral part of the 1922 and 1923 championship winning sides. Lacey left the club in 1924, moving to New Brighton, before winding his career up at Shelbourne.

Elisha Scott

Games: 467

Years: 22

Liverpool's longest serving player, 19 year old goalkeeper Elisha Scott was signed by Tom Watson in 1912 following a recommendation by Scott's older brother Billy, with the Belfast boy going on to spend more than twenty years at the club. He made his debut against Newcastle at St James' Park on New Year's Day 1913, and by all accounts was so impressive that Newcastle offered Liverpool £1,000 for him there and then. Fortunately for all at Anfield, the bid was rejected, and Scott played 467 times for Liverpool before departing, his final game coming on February 21, 1934. Returning to his native Northern Ireland he became player-manager of Belfast Celtic, winning 10 Irish League titles and 6 Irish Cups. Elisha Scott died on May 16, 1959, aged just 64.

Match fixing

On Good Friday 1915, Manchester United played Liverpool at Old Trafford. Manchester United were fighting for their lives in a relegation battle, whilst Liverpool were sliding into mid-table obscurity. It had become apparent to everyone involved in English football that the First World War was to lead to a suspension of league football at the end of the 1914-1915 season. The match ended in a 2-0 win for the hosts, Liverpool missing a penalty in a performance which was noted by observers, and the match referee, as surprisingly lacklustre.

Following the game, allegations were made that a large bet had been placed on Manchester United to win 2-0 at odds of 7/1. A Football League investigation was launched which culminated in life bans for seven players, Sandy Turnbull, Arthur Whalley and Enoch West of Manchester United, and Jackie Sheldon, Tom Miller, Bob Pursell and Thomas Fairfoul of Liverpool. The plot, orchestrated by Sheldon, was opposed by some other players such as Fred Pagnam, who hit the crossbar late in the game, causing his team mates to remonstrate with him on the pitch, and later testified against the conspirators.

Harry "Smiler" Chambers
1915-1928

Nicknamed "Smiler", Harry Chambers was born in Willington Quay, Northumberland on December 17, 1896, but it was on Merseyside rather than his native Tyneside that he was to make his name. Averaging just less than a goal every other game, Chambers would command an astronomical fee in the modern era, his powerful left foot shot firing Liverpool to league titles in 1922 and 1923. He made 339 appearances and scored 151 goals for Liverpool before his transfer to West Bromwich Albion at the age of 32, and he continued to play football at some level for another twenty years, his career as player-manager of Shropshire side Oakengates Town only being ended by his death in 1949 at the age of 52.

Stats: Position: Striker. Years: 13. Games: 339. Goals: 151.

MANAGERS

David Ashworth
1919-1922

David Ashworth was already an experienced manager by the time he took the Liverpool job, having spent eight largely successful years with Oldham Athletic, and five as the manager of Stockport County. He joined Liverpool in December 1919, taking over from George Patterson who had left following a run of just two wins in 11 games. Under Ashworth's stewardship the team had a strong second half to the season, finishing in fourth place, following that up with a second fourth place finish in 1920-21, and then with Liverpool's third league title in 1922. December 1922 saw Ashworth controversially leave a Liverpool side flying high at the top of the league to rejoin his first club Oldham, mired in relegation troubles at the foot of the table. By all accounts this was for personal reasons, his wife and daughter, both invalids, lived in a house in Stockport, 11 miles from Oldham but 43 miles from Liverpool. Ashworth's Oldham team were relegated in 1923.

MANAGERS

Matt McQueen
1922-1928

A former Liverpool player who had actually appeared in every single outfield position for the club between 1892 and 1899, as well as turning out in goal twelve times, Matt McQueen took charge when David Ashworth resigned from the manager's job in December 1922. Initially taking the job on a temporary basis, he helped the club to clinch their second successive title, and kept the job for a further five years, becoming the first former Liverpool player to manage the club. Although the remainder of his tenure was largely unremarkable, he did sign one of Liverpool's greatest ever players in Gordon Hodgson. Whilst on a scouting mission to Sheffield he was involved in a car accident in which he lost a leg, and the resultant ill health forced his retirement in 1928. Matt McQueen died in September 1944 at the age of 81.

GORDON HODGSON

Forward

233 Goals

358 Games

11 Years (1925-1936)

One of Anfield's earliest heroes, Gordon Hodgson hailed from South Africa, but the burly Johannesburg native made his home in Lancashire. Strong, quick, and with a rocket of a shot, Hodgson scored 233 goals in 358 games for Liverpool between 1925 and 1936. As well as turning out for Liverpool, Hodgson played 56 first-class cricket matches for Lancashire, taking 148 wickets as a right arm fast bowler and twice winning the County Championship. During his time at Anfield, Hodgson scored 17 hat-tricks, a club record which stands to this day. He left the club to sign for Aston Villa in January 1936 for the princely sum of £3,000. Hodgson died of cancer on June 14, 1951, at the age of just 47.

MANAGERS

George Kay
1936-1951

The man who signed Bob Paisley and Billy Liddell, George Kay joined Liverpool from Southampton in the summer of 1936. He had an inauspicious start to his Liverpool career, with just three wins and four draws from the first twelve games, and his first few seasons were largely anonymous, finishing 18th in his first and 11th in the two following. The signings of Paisley and Liddell came in preparation for the 1939-40 season, but with league football suspended for the duration of the Second World War it wasn't until 1946 that Kay could really put his new team to the test. That team performed remarkably, winning Liverpool's first title since 1923. Kay's team would never reach such heights again and he retired through ill health in 1951, passing away three years later at the age of 62.

Billy Liddell

A player so influential that the club became known as "Liddellpool", Billy Liddell was born in Townhill, Fife, on January 10, 1922. Known for his powerful physique, turn of pace and ability to let fly from all angles, Liddell joined Liverpool as an amateur on July 27, 1938, signing professional forms the following year on wages of £3 a week. Although the Second World War prevented him from making his official Liverpool debut, he guested for various select teams throughout the war. Between his debut on January 5, 1946 and his retirement in 1961, Billy Liddell played 534 games for Liverpool, scoring 228 goals. A winger whose versatility allowed him to play both inside and centre forward, after his retirement Liddell became a Justice of the Peace, bursar of Liverpool University, and heavily involved in voluntary work. Billy Liddell died in Liverpool on July 3, 2001.

LAURIE HUGHES
Defender
303 Games
14 Years (1943-1957)

The first Liverpool player to play in a World Cup, Laurie Hughes joined the club in 1943. Previously a Tranmere trainee, Hughes made his Liverpool debut on January 5, 1946, in a 2-0 FA Cup 3rd Round victory over Chester. He was an important part of the 1946-47 title winning team, and was chosen to represent England at the 1950 World Cup in Brazil, replacing the departing Neil Franklin. He played all three games of England's World Cup, including the famous 1-0 defeat by the USA, as England crashed out of the tournament at the group stages. Sustaining a bad injury during the 1950 Charity Shield match between England and a Canadian XI, he played no more games for England, and whilst he remained an important part of Liverpool's team, he was never to reach those heights again. He was part of the Liverpool team which was relegated in 1954, and finally played his last game for Liverpool in 1957, aged 33.

"SIR" ROGER HUNT

286 GOALS

492 GAMES

11 YEARS (1958-1969)

286 goals in 492 games marks "Sir" Roger Hunt out as one of Liverpool's greatest ever goalscorers. Signed by Phil Taylor on July 29, 1958, Hunt made his debut, and got his debut goal, against Scunthorpe that September, the first of 245 league goals in a Liverpool shirt, still a club record. Taylor was replaced by Shankly, who began to rebuild Liverpool as a club, and one with Roger Hunt at its heart. Fast, strong, and with an unparalleled work rate, Sir Roger may be remembered across the country for his role as Geoff Hurst's partner in the 1966 World Cup Final, but the diminutive Hunt's name lives longer on the Kop for his domestic exploits between 1958 and '69 than for anything in an England jersey.

Bill Shankly
1959-1974

The man who built Liverpool, Bill Shankly arrived at Anfield on Monday December 14, 1959. The club had been languishing in the Second Division for five years, and had just been knocked out of the FA Cup by non-league Worcester City. Anfield was falling apart, the Melwood training ground was overgrown, and the squad was filled with players Shankly deemed no good, twenty four of whom he transfer listed and sold within his first year. Shankly's reign at Liverpool is now the stuff of legend, as he guided the club to the Second Division title in 1962, First Division titles in 1964, 1966 and 1973, FA Cup wins in 1965 and 1974, and the 1973 UEFA Cup. Shankly's legacy at Liverpool is not just to be seen in the trophy cabinet, however. His influence can be felt in every corner of the club, from the pride taken in attractive passing football to the close connection between the club's supporters and their manager. Shankly died on September 29, 1981, seven years after leaving Anfield, the club erecting the famous Shankly Gates in his honour.

Stats: Position: Manager. Years: 15.

RON YEATS

Centre Half

454 Games

10 Years (1961-1971)

The captain of the first truly great Liverpool team of the 1960s, Bill Shankly brought Ron Yeats to Liverpool in 1961 for £20,000 from Dundee United. Yeats went on to make 454 appearances for Liverpool over the next decade, becoming the longest serving captain in the history of the club and the first Liverpool captain to lift the FA Cup. The former slaughterhouse worker from Aberdeen was one of Liverpool's most inspirational players, the heart of the team which took Liverpool from Second Division also-rans to one of the biggest teams in Europe. He left Anfield in 1971 to become player-manager of Tranmere, continuing to ply his trade in the lower leagues until his final retirement in 1978.

Written by Rodgers and Hammerstein for the musical *Carousel*, and scoring a number one for Gerry and the Pacemakers in 1963, over the following half century the strains of "You'll Never Walk Alone", sung by the massed ranks of the Kop, have become synonymous with Liverpool Football Club. Gerry Marsden, leader of the Pacemakers, gave a copy to Bill Shankly prior to its release and the rest, as they say, is history. Following Liverpool's lead, numerous clubs have since adopted it as their anthem, including Celtic, Feyenoord, FC Twente, Borussia Dortmund, Club Brugge and FC Tokyo, but there's only one place it really sounds right, Anfield.

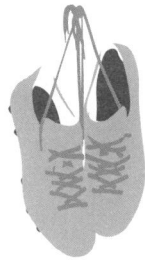

The Boot Room

When Bill Shankly arrived at Liverpool in December 1959, he set about rebuilding the entire football club from the ground up. The heart and soul, the foundations, the whole base around which his football club would be built was the Boot Room. Shankly, Bob Paisley, Joe Fagan, Reuben Bennett and latterly Tom Saunders formed the core of that first boot room, and through it Liverpool built a managerial production line, developing managers ingrained with Liverpool's style and ethos, and geared towards Liverpool's success. Beyond the direct effect on Paisley and Fagan, the Boot Room shaped the careers of Kenny Dalglish and Roy Evans, Shankly's influence being felt around Anfield to the end of the Twentieth Century and beyond.

FA Cup Final Wembley Stadium, London

01/05/1965 / Liverpool vs Leeds United

Liverpool /
Lawrence, Lawler, Byrne, Strong, Yeats, Stevenson, Callaghan, Smith, Thompson, Hunt, St John.

Leeds United /
Sprake, Reaney, Bell, Charlton, Hunter, Collins, Bremner, Giles, Johanneson, Storrie, Peacock.

Liverpool 2-1 Leeds United
(Hunt, 93, Bremner, 100, St John, 113)

Liverpool's first FA Cup victory was only sealed after extra time, with Ian St John's diving header handing Bill Shankly's side the famous trophy. The midfield axis of Bobby Collins and Billy Bremner which had guided Leeds to 2nd in the league table failed to fire, and Liverpool's strike partnership of St John and Hunt scored the decisive goals which ensured the trophy made its way to Merseyside.

EMLYN HUGHES

49 GOALS

665 GAMES

12 YEARS (1967-1979)

The first Liverpool captain to lift the European Cup, Barrow born Emlyn Hughes signed for Liverpool from Blackpool in 1967 for £65,000. He would go on to captain Liverpool and England, and make 665 appearances for the Reds over 12 years. Moving from midfield, to full back, and finally to centre half, Hughes became the heartbeat of Shankly's team and the foundation upon which all of Liverpool's success during the 1970s was built. He won four league titles, an FA Cup, two UEFA Cups and two European Cups at Liverpool, before leaving for Wolverhampton Wanderers where he picked up the League Cup, the only trophy which had eluded him during his time at Anfield. Emlyn Hughes died on November 9, 2004, aged just 57.

Ray Clemence

Games: 665
Years: 14

Joining Liverpool from Scunthorpe in 1967, Ray Clemence would go on to make 665 appearances for the club, becoming one of the best goalkeepers in Europe in the process. During his time at Liverpool Clemence won 5 league titles, 3 European Cups, 2 UEFA Cups, an FA Cup and a League Cup. Costing just £18,000, Clemence must go down as one of Bill Shankly's greatest bargains. He collected 61 England caps, a number which would have been vastly higher had he not had to compete against Peter Shilton for the number 1 shirt. Clemence left Liverpool in 1981, with Tottenham Hotspur paying £300,000 for his services, and he would play for another 7 years before retiring.

KEVIN KEEGAN

| Forward |
| 100 Goals |
| 323 Games |
| 6 Years (1971-1977) |

An icon who defined English football in the 1970s, Kevin Keegan arrived at Liverpool in 1971 for £35,000. A 20 year old who had played most of his football for first club Scunthorpe on the right of midfield, Bill Shankly quickly recognised the Doncaster lad's attacking prowess and shifted him up front to partner John Toshack. Marking his debut against Nottingham Forest with a goal after 12 minutes, Keegan went on to score 100 goals in 323 games for the club before departing for Hamburg for half a million pounds in 1977. During his time at Liverpool he won three league titles, two UEFA Cups, one FA Cup and Liverpool's first European Cup.

UEFA Cup Final First Leg
Anfield, Liverpool

10/05/1973 / Liverpool vs Borussia Monchengladbach

Liverpool /
Clemence, Lawler, Lindsay, Lloyd, Hughes, Callaghan, Heighway, Smith, Cormack, Toshack, Keegan.
Subs / Lane, Storton, Thompson, Hall (Heighway, 83), Boersma.

Borussia Monchengladbach /
Kleff, Michallik, Vogts, Netzer, Bonhof, Wimmer, Danner, Kulik, Jensen, Rupp, Heynckes.
Subs / Simonsen (Rupp, 82).

Liverpool 3-0 Borussia Monchengladbach
(Keegan, 21, Keegan, 32, Lloyd, 61)

The first leg of the 1973 UEFA Cup Final had been scheduled for May 9, but heavy rain in Liverpool meant that the referee postponed the game after just 27 minutes of play. The replay the following evening saw the introduction of John Toshack in place of Brian Hall, and it was the Welshman's header across the box which set up Kevin Keegan's first goal of the night, and put Liverpool on course for a resounding aggregate lead.

UEFA Cup Final Second Leg
Bokelbergstadion, Monchengladbach

23/05/1973 / Borussia Monchengladbach vs Liverpool

Borussia Monchengladbach /
Kleff, Surau, Vogts, Netzer, Bonhof, Wimmer, Danner, Kulik, Jensen, Rupp, Heynckes.
Subs / Schrage, Michallik, Sieloff, Simonsen.

Liverpool /
Clemence, Lawler, Lindsay, Lloyd, Hughes, Callaghan, Heighway, Smith, Cormack, Toshack Keegan.
Subs / Lane, Storton, Thompson, Hall, Boersma (Heighway, 77).

Borussia Monchengladbach 2-0 Liverpool
(Heynckes, 29, Heynckes, 40)

Played just over a fortnight after the first leg, Liverpool's commanding 3-0 lead forced Borussia to go on the offensive, something which they did with aplomb, Jupp Heynckes putting his side 2-0 up before the break. Unfortunately for Borussia they couldn't find that vital third goal, and Liverpool held on to win their first European trophy, and become the first English club to win a European trophy and a domestic title in the same season.

FA Cup Final Wembley Stadium, London

04/05/1974 / Liverpool vs Newcastle United

Liverpool /
Clemence, Smith, Lindsay, Thompson, Hughes, Callaghan, Heighway, Cormack, Hall, Keegan, Toshack.
Subs / Lawler.

Newcastle United /
McFaul, Clark, Kennedy, Howard, Moncur, Smith, Hibbitt, McDermott, Cassidy, MacDonald, Tudor.
Subs / Gibb (Smith, 70).

Liverpool 3-0 Newcastle United
(Keegan, 57, Heighway, 74, Keegan, 88)

Bill Shankly's final match as Liverpool manager saw his side roundly defeat a Newcastle team containing future Liverpool stalwarts Alan Kennedy and Terry McDermott. Liverpool had finished the season in second place behind Don Revie's Leeds, but Newcastle ended the year in 15th, just two points clear of the relegation places, and the gulf in class between the sides was all too obvious. Kevin Keegan's goals against the club with which he would go on to be synonymous took the famous trophy back to Merseyside for the second time.

Bob Paisley
1939-1992

'If you're in the penalty area and don't know what to do with the ball, put it in the net and we'll discuss the options later.'

-Bob Paisley

Born in Hetton-le-Hole, County Durham, on January 23, 1919, Bob Paisley spent over fifty years at Liverpool as a player, physiotherapist, coach, assistant manager, and finally as arguably the greatest manager the club has ever known. Taking over after the resignation of Bill Shankly in 1974, during his nine seasons in charge Paisley won six league titles, three League Cups, 1 UEFA Cup, 1 European Super Cup, 5 Charity Shields, and became the first man to win three European Cups. Retiring from management at the end of the 1982-83 season, Paisley acted as an advisor to Kenny Dalglish during the first two years of his tenure, before becoming a club director, a role he retained until 1992. Bob Paisley died on Valentine's Day 1996, aged 77, and was honoured, as his friend Bill Shankly had been, with a set of gates at Anfield.

Stats: Position: Defender. Years: 15. **Position:** Coach and Physiotherapist. Years: 5. **Position:** Assistant Manager. Years: 15. **Position:** Assistant Manager. Years: 9. **Position:** Advisor. Years: 2. **Position:** Club Director. Years: 7.

UEFA Cup Final First Leg
Anfield, Liverpool

28/04/1976 / Liverpool vs Club Brugge

Liverpool /
Clemence, Neal, Smith, Thompson, Hughes, Heighway, Kennedy, Callaghan, Toshack, Fairclough, Keegan.
Subs / McDonnell, Jones, Hall, McDermott, Case (Toshack, 46).

Club Brugge /
Jensen, Bastijns, Volders, Krieger, Leekens, Vandereycken, Cools, de Cubber, Gool, Lambert, le Fevre.

Liverpool 3-2 Club Brugge
(Lambert, 5, Cools, 15, Kennedy, 59, Case, 61, Keegan, 65)

Liverpool fought back from 2-0 down to edge this first leg clash with a side on the way to a Belgian title win. An early mistake by Phil Neal allowed Raoul Lambert to score after 5 minutes, with the impeccably named Julien Cools extending the Belgians lead on 15. Liverpool's second half comeback left the tie precariously poised.

UEFA Cup Final Second Leg
Olympiastadion, Brugge

19/05/1976 / Club Brugge vs Liverpool

Club Brugge /
Jansen, Bastijns, Volders, Krieger, Leekens, Cools, Vandereycken, de Cubber, van Gool, Lambert, le Fevre.
Subs / Sanders (Lambert, 75), Hinderyckx (de Cubber, 68)

Liverpool /
Clemence, Neal, Smith, Thompson, Hughes, Heighway, Kennedy, Case, Callaghan, Toshack, Keegan.
Subs / McDonnell, Jones, Hall, McDermott, Fairclough (Toshack, 62).

Club Brugge 1-1 Liverpool
(Lambert pen, 11, Keegan, 15)

Liverpool went to Brugge with a slender first-leg lead, with the Belgians knowing that a win by just one clear goal would prevent the trophy returning to Anfield. Brugge went ahead through an early penalty, before being pegged back by Kevin Keegan. The second half was described by Bob Paisley as "the longest 45 minutes of my life", but his boys held their nerve and the UEFA Cup returned to Liverpool for a second time.

European Cup Final Stadio Olimpico, Rome

25/05/1977 / Liverpool vs Borussia Monchengladbach

Liverpool /
Clemence, Neal, Jones, Smith, Hughes, Callaghan, Kennedy, Case, McDermott, Heighway, Keegan.
Subs / McDonnell, Fairclough, Johnson, Waddle, Lindsay

Borussia Monchengladbach /
Kneib, Vogts, Klinkhammer, Wittkamp, Bonhof, Wohlers, Simonsen, Wimmer, Stielike, Schafer, Heynckes.
Subs / Kleff, Hannes (Wohlers, 79), Kulik (Wimmer, 24), Del'Haye, Heidenreich.

Liverpool 3-1 Borussia Monchengladbach
(McDermott, 28, Simonsen, 52, Smith, 64, Neal, 82)

Liverpool's first European Cup triumph came in front of 57,000 at the Stadio Olimpico in Rome. A replay of the 1973 UEFA Cup Final, it was the first time that either Liverpool or Borussia had reached the European Cup Final. Liverpool and Borussia both entered the game as domestic champions, but it was the Anfield side who came out on top with Tommy Smith scoring to mark his 600th game for the club.

"King" Kenny Dalglish - The Player
1977-1990

The greatest of many great players to grace the Anfield turf.

Kevin Keegan's departure from Anfield left a pretty sizeable pair of boots to fill, and it was with some scepticism that Liverpool fans received the club's replacement, Kenneth Mathieson Dalglish. Signed from Celtic for a British record £440,000, the man they would call the "King" would go on to be the greatest of the many great players to grace the Anfield turf. Scoring on his league debut against Middlesbrough on August 13, 1977, Dalglish would go on to notch 31 times in his first season, and 172 in 515 games for Liverpool as player and player-manager.

Stats: Position: Centre Forward. Years: 12. Games: 515. Goals: 172.

ALAN HANSEN
14 GOALS
620 GAMES
13 YEARS (1977-1991)

The first outfield player to win the English league title in three different decades, Alan Hansen was born in Sauchie, Clackmannanshire on June 13, 1955. Beginning his professional career at Partick Thistle, Bob Paisley brought Hansen to Anfield for £110,000 in the summer of 1977. Making his debut on September 24 against Derby County at Anfield, Hansen was in and out of the team, not fully establishing himself as first choice centre half until Emlyn Hughes departed for Wolverhampton Wanderers in 1979. He would remain at Liverpool until 1991, retiring a month after Kenny Dalglish's resignation as manager. Hansen made 620 appearances for Liverpool, scoring 14 goals, winning eight league titles and three European Cups.

European Cup Final
Wembley Stadium, London

10/05/1978 / Liverpool vs Club Brugge

Liverpool /
Clemence, Neal, Hansen, Thompson, Hughes, Case, Kennedy, McDermott, Souness, Fairclough, Dalglish.
Subs / Ogrizovic, Jones, Irwin, Callaghan, Heighway (Case, 63).

Club Brugge /
Jensen, Bastijns, Krieger, Leekens, Maes, Cools, Vandereycken, De Cubber, Simoen, Ku, Sorensen.
Subs / Sanders (Ku, 58), Volders (Maes, 80).

Liverpool 1-0 Club Brugge
(Dalglish, 64)

Kenny Dalglish finished his first season as a Liverpool player in style with the winning goal in the 1978 European Cup Final. Liverpool retained the trophy in front of a capacity crowd at Wembley Stadium, Dalglish's goal being enough to see them through against a Brugge team Bob Paisley said "only seemed to be concerned with keeping the score down".

IAN RUSH

Striker

346 Goals

660 Games

15 Years (1980-1987, 1988-1996)

346 goals in 660 appearances over two spells at the club marks Ian Rush out as one of Liverpool's greatest forwards. Joining from Chester City for £300,000 in 1980, Rush took 9 games to get his first goal, but it was to be the first of many in red. Making his way from callow youth to the mainstay of the Liverpool front line alongside Kenny Dalglish, Rush's remarkable goalscoring exploits saw him win PFA Young Player of the Year, PFA Player of the Year, Football Writers Footballer of the Year and BBC Wales Sports Personality of the Year, before departing for Juventus in 1987. After a year in Turin, apocryphally described as "like living in a foreign country", Rush returned to Liverpool in 1988, remaining at the club until 1996. During his time at Liverpool, Ian Rush won 5 titles, 5 League Cups, 3 FA Cups and 2 European Cups, as well as being the club's top scorer for a staggering 9 seasons.

European Cup Final Parc des Princes, Paris

27/05/1981 / Real Madrid vs Liverpool

Roma /
Rodriguez, Cortes, Camacho, Sabido, Garcia Navajas, Stielike, Del Bosque, de los Santos, Cunningham, Juanito, Santillana.
Subs / Gonzalez, San Jose, Angel, Hernandez, Pineda (Cortes, 87).

Liverpool /
Clemence, Neal, A. Kennedy, Hansen, Thompson, Lee, R. Kennedy, McDermott, Souness, Johnson, Dalglish.
Subs / Ogrizovic, Irwin, Money, Case (Dalglish, 85), Gayle.

Real Madrid 0-1 Liverpool
(A. Kennedy, 82)

The 1981 European Cup Final pitted Liverpool against the most successful side in the history of the competition. Real Madrid were taking part in their ninth final, with six wins to Liverpool's two, but the trophy would be heading back to Anfield once more. Alan Kennedy's late winner sent the travelling Liverpool fans into raptures as Bob Paisley became the first manager to win the European Cup three times.

Joe Fagan
1958-1985

After a playing career spent largely at Manchester City, Joe Fagan joined Liverpool in 1958 as a coach, 18 months before Bill Shankly's arrival at the club. An integral part of the Boot Room, Fagan moved through the coaching ranks at the club, from the reserves to the first team and then, following Bob Paisley's retirement in 1983, to the manager's office. Fagan spent two years as Liverpool manager, from July 1983 to May 1985, winning an unprecedented treble of league title, League Cup and European Cup. On May 29, 1985, just hours before the Heysel Stadium disaster, Fagan announced his retirement from football, to be replaced by player-manager Kenny Dalglish. Joe Fagan died on June 30, 2001, and was buried at Anfield Cemetery.

Stats: Position: Coach. Years: 15. **Position:** Manager. Years: 2.

European Cup Final Stadio Olimpico, Rome

30/05/1984 / Roma vs Liverpool

Roma /
Tancredi, Nappi, Bonetti, Nela, Righetti, Di Bartolomei, Falcao, Cerezo, Conti, Pruzzo, Graziani.
Subs / Malgioglio, Oddi, Strukelj (Cerezo, 115), Chierico (Pruzzo, 64), Vincenzi.

Liverpool /
Grobbelaar, Neal, Kennedy, Hansen, Lawrenson, Lee, Whelan, Johnston, Souness, Dalglish, Rush.
Subs / Bolder, Gillespie, Nicol (Johnston, 72), Hodgson, Robinson (Dalglish, 94).

Roma 1-1 Liverpool
(Neal, 13, Pruzzo, 42). Liverpool win 4-2 on penalties.

Joe Fagan's Liverpool went to Rome in 1984 and won their fourth European Cup the hard way, defeating Roma on home turf at the Stadio Olimpico. The site of the club's 1977 triumph was to be glorious once more as Liverpool, and the famously wobbly legs of Bruce Grobbelaar, won a tightly contested final 4-2 on penalties.

JAN MOLBY

Central Midfielder

61 Goals

292 Games

12 Years (1984-1996)

The kind of player you pay your money to watch on a Saturday afternoon, Jan Molby was signed from Ajax by Joe Fagan on August 22, 1984, and would go on to play 292 games in a Liverpool shirt scoring 61 goals. Not the most athletic footballer in the world, Molby was blessed with a grace and vision which allowed him to unlock many a defence, and made him a favourite with the Anfield faithful. Beset by injuries and issues with his fitness, he probably did not play as many games as his unquestionable ability deserved, but he was a joy to watch with the ball at his feet, and scored some truly spectacular goals.

Kenny Dalglish - The Manager
1985-1991, 2011-2012

Taking over as player-manager after Joe Fagan's resignation, and in the wake of the Heysel disaster, the Kop's greatest hero had what looked like an insurmountable challenge on his hands. However, just as Kenny had stepped in and replaced Kevin Keegan on the pitch, so he took up the mantle of Shankly, Paisley and Fagan off it, leading the club to its first ever league and FA Cup double in his debut season as player-manager. As Liverpool's manager, Dalglish won three league titles and two FA Cups, but beyond that success he was an enormous presence in the aftermath of Hillsborough, attending the funerals of many of the victims, including four in one day. It is for this compassion, for this empathy in a time of tragedy, as much as for his achievements as player or manager, that Dalglish is loved by Liverpool fans. Resigning on health grounds in 1991, he went on to manage Blackburn Rovers, Newcastle and Celtic, before returning to the Liverpool manager's job in 2011, adding the 2012 League Cup to his list of achievements.

Stats: Position: Manager. Years: 7.

FA Cup Final Wembley Stadium, London

05/10/1986 / Liverpool vs Everton

Liverpool /
Grobbelaar, Nicol, Beglin, Lawrenson, Hansen, Johnston, Whelan, Molby, MacDonald, Dalglish, Rush.
Subs / Steve McMahon.

Everton /
Mimms, Stevens, Van Den Hauwe, Ratcliffe, Mountfield, Bracewell, Sheedy, Reid, Steven, Lineker, Sharp.
Subs / Heath (Stevens, 72).

Liverpool 3-1 Everton
(Lineker, 27, Rush, 56, Johnston, 62, Rush, 83)

The 1986 FA Cup Final was a Merseyside derby, title winners Liverpool and league runners-up Everton clashing at Wembley. Ian Rush cancelled out Gary Lineker's opening goal early in the second half and player-manager Kenny Dalglish's side went on to lift the famous trophy for the first time in 12 years.

John Barnes
1987-1997

"The future of English Football"
-Zico

Once described by Zico as "the future of English football", John Barnes joined Liverpool in the summer of 1987 for £900,000. Already a proven top-flight footballer with Watford, Barnes would go on to even greater heights, being voted PFA Player of the Year in his first season at the club as Liverpool romped to the title. A career split by injury, from the livewire of the late '80s to the more measured, mature and cultured midfield player of the 1990s, Barnes proved his ability in a Liverpool shirt time and again. In all, he played 407 games for Liverpool, scoring 108 goals, before leaving the club to link up with Kenny Dalglish at Newcastle United.

Stats: Position: Left winger. Years: 10. Games: 407. Goals: 108.

15.04.1989

96 killed, 766 injured, April 15, 1989 was the greatest tragedy in the history of Liverpool Football Club, and one which would change the face of English football forever. The 1980s had seen a number of potential disasters avoided, including a crush at Hillsborough in Sheffield in 1981 during a game between Tottenham and Wycombe which had seen 38 injured. After the 1981 crush a number of changes were made to the Leppings Lane end, including separating the terrace into pens, but the ground's safety certificate and capacity were not updated.

On the day of the tragedy, as large numbers of fans waited outside the Hillsborough ground to see Liverpool play Nottingham Forest in the FA Cup semi-final, three exit gates were opened. The fans outside entered the ground, pouring into the central pen, filling it beyond capacity. Whilst ordinarily police or stewards would have been present to direct fans to the outer pens, for some reason this was not the case. At 3:06pm the referee stopped the match as fans climbed the fences to escape the crush. Fans between the ages of 10 and 67 were killed, fatalities of a disastrous failure of the authorities to protect fans, one described by the Hillsborough Independent Panel as showing a "lack of police control" and crowd safety "compromised at every level".

It was a watershed moment in English football, the Taylor report triggering the introduction of all seater stadia and bringing a tragic end to one of the darkest decades in the history of the English game.

FA Cup Final Wembley Stadium, London

20/05/1989 / Liverpool vs Everton

Liverpool /
Grobbelaar, Staunton, Nicol, Ablett, Hansen, Barnes, Houghton, Whelan, McMahon, Beardsley, Aldridge.
Subs / Venison (Staunton, 90), Rush (Aldridge, 73).

Everton /
Southall, McDonald, Van Den Hauwe, Ratcliffe, Watson, Nevin, Sheedy, Bracewell, Steven, Cottee, Sharp.
Subs / Wilson (Sheedy, 78), McCall (Bracewell, 59).

Liverpool 3-2 Everton
(Aldridge, 4, McCall, 89, Rush, 95, McCall, 102, Rush, 104)

A final played in the most emotional of circumstances, a mere five weeks after the Hillsborough disaster, it was the second Merseyside final, one in which substitute Ian Rush secured the famous trophy for Liverpool just as he had done in the corresponding fixture in 1986. It was a victory Kenny Dalglish described as his greatest triumph, the resilience of his players a fitting tribute to the victims of the club's greatest tragedy.

Graham Souness
1991-1994

Sacked

The reign of Graeme Souness as Liverpool manager, taking over from Kenny Dalglish in 1991 and lasting until his sacking in 1994, is not one remembered with much fondness by Liverpool fans. Demolishing the Boot Room, giving an interview to *The Sun* on the third anniversary of Hillsborough, constant reports of fights with staff and club legends, Souness was the first Liverpool manager to be sacked since Don Welsh in 1956. His tenure was not without positives, however, with an FA Cup Final victory over Sunderland in 1992 and the introduction of young players like Steve McManaman and Robbie Fowler into the first team.

Stats: Position: Manager. Years: 3.

STEVE McMANAMAN

66 GOALS

364 GAMES

9 YEARS (1990-1999)

The quintessential Spice Boy, Steve McManaman may have left Liverpool under a cloud, but his influence on the Liverpool team of the 1990s, as well as his personal achievements as a footballer, cannot be underestimated. Making his debut in a 2-0 victory over Sheffield United on December 15, 1990, McManaman was the youngest player on the pitch in Liverpool's FA Cup Final win in 1992, winning the Man of the Match award after setting up Michael Thomas for Liverpool's opening goal. McManaman was to become synonymous with Liverpool during the 1990s, granted more and more freedom by Roy Evans, scoring twice in the 1995 League Cup Final.

He remained a pivotal player in Liverpool's side, and one of the most exciting players in the Premier League, but contract disputes lead to his departure to Real Madrid in 1999, after 364 games and 66 goals for Liverpool. He went on to become the first English footballer to win the Champions League with a non-English club, and won the most overseas trophies of any English footballer.

FA Cup Final Wembley Stadium, London

09/05/1992 / Liverpool vs Sunderland

Liverpool /
Grobbelaar, Jones, Burrows, Nicol, Wright, Houghton, McManaman, Molby, Thomas, Rush, Saunders.
Subs / Marsh, Walters.

Sunderland /
Norman, Owers, Rogan, Ball, Bennett, Atkinson, Rush, Bracewell, Armstrong, Davenport, Byrne.
Subs / Hardyman (Rush, 69), Hawke (Armstrong, 77).

Liverpool 2-0 Sunderland
(Thomas, 47, Rush, 68)

In the first final to feature a Second Division team since 1982, Liverpool collected their only major trophy under the management of Graeme Souness, with second half goals from Michael Thomas and Ian Rush ending Sunderland's hopes of winning their first FA Cup Final since 1973. During the medal presentation the sides were actually presented with the wrong medals, the Sunderland team receiving Liverpool's winners medals, leaving the players to swap the medals themselves on the pitch.

ROBBIE FOWLER

Centre Forward
183 Goals
369 Games
10 Years (1991-2001, 2003)

In the beginning, there was the Word, and the Word was "Robbie Fowler". Born in Toxteth on April 9, 1975, Robert Bernard Fowler is one of the most natural centre forwards England has ever produced. Immensely gifted, with an instinctive ability to put the ball in the back of the net, Fowler signed youth forms with the club in 1991, and made his debut in League Cup tie against Fulham on September 22, 1993, scoring to round off a 3-1 victory over the Cottagers. A key part of Liverpool's team throughout the 1990s, Fowler left the club for £12m in 2001 to join Leeds United. Although he returned to Anfield in 2006, he could not rekindle the magic of his earlier years, and left after just one season. In all, the man they called "God" appeared 369 times for Liverpool over the two spells, scoring 183 goals.

MANAGERS

Roy Evans
1994-1998

The last of the Boot Room graduates, Roy Evans took over from Graeme Souness in 1994, the culmination of more than 30 years at Anfield. The club's solitary honour during his tenure was the 1995 League Cup, the game which became affectionately known by Liverpool fans as "The McManaman Final" after Liverpool won 2-1 with a pair of goals from the talismanic midfielder. Evans would go on to mould his team around McManaman, as well as giving a first team debut to Michael Owen, before his departure in 1998 after four ill-fated months of co-management with Gerard Houllier.

JAMIE CARRAGHER

DEFENDER

700 GAMES

17 YEARS (1996-2013)

More than 700 appearances in a red shirt, 17 years at the club, there are few players more synonymous with Liverpool than Jamie Carragher. The Bootle born boy signed professional forms with the club in October 1996, making his first team debut under Roy Evans on January 8, 1997. Carragher's versatility, his willingness to play three or four different positions, meant that he quickly established himself as part of the Liverpool squad, and meant he was fast-tracked into the England setup by Kevin Keegan. This versatility also worked against him, both at club and international level, as he struggled to nail down a single position until Rafa Benitez arrived, shifting Carragher to centre half. Widely acknowledged as one of the best central defenders the Premier League has seen, Carragher collected 2 FA Cups, 3 League Cups, UEFA Cup and Champions League winners medals during his time at the club.

Gerard Houllier
1998-2004

Gerard Houllier joined Liverpool as co-manager ... a situation which always seemed destined for disaster.

The first man from outside the British Isles to step into the Anfield hot-seat, Gerard Houllier joined Liverpool as co-manager with Roy Evans in the summer of 1998, a situation which always seemed destined for disaster. Indeed, Evans departed in November, leaving Houllier in sole charge to oversee yet another transitional period in a decade of transitional periods. A significant turnover of players, a conscious attempt to shift away from the Spice Boys era, and a modernising drive off the pitch left him at odds with many Liverpool fans, yet his era saw the club collect a treble of the FA Cup, League Cup and UEFA Cup in 2001, the League Cup in 2003, as well as finishing 2nd in the Premier League in 2002, Liverpool's highest league finish since 1991. A period of ill health caused by a heart complaint saw Phil Thompson step in as caretaker manager between October 2001 and February 2002, before Houllier was ready to return to management. He left the club by mutual consent in 2004.

Stats: Position: Co-manager. Years: 0.41. **Position:** Manager. Years: 6.

Steven Gerrard

Born May 30, 1980, the same month that Liverpool clinched their twelfth title, nobody could have known the impact that Steven Gerrard was to have on the club. Growing up in Whiston, and playing first for Whiston Juniors, Gerrard joined the Liverpool academy at the age of nine. Making his first team debut against Blackburn Rovers on November 29, 1998, Gerrard made thirteen appearances in his first season. Little did anyone know that that gangly youth would go on to become one of the most complete midfielders in the world, captain of his club and country, and one of the greatest players ever to grace the Anfield turf. Would anyone bet against him following in the footsteps of Messrs. Shankly, Paisley and Fagan once he finally hangs up his boots?

FA Cup Final Millennium Stadium, Cardiff

12/05/2001 / Arsenal vs Liverpool

Arsenal /
Seaman, Dixon, Cole, Keown, Adams, Pires, Ljungberg, Grimandi, Vieira, Wiltord, Henry.
Subs / Manninger, Lauren, Parlour (Wiltord, 76), Bergkamp (Dixon, 90), Kanu (Ljungberg, 85).

Liverpool /
Westerveld, Babbel, Carragher, Henchoz, Hyypia, Murphy, Smicer, Gerrard, Hamann, Heskey, Owen.
Subs / Arphexad, Vignal, Berger (Murphy, 77), McAllister (Hamann, 60), Fowler, (Smicer, 77).

Arsenal 1-2 Liverpool
(Ljungberg, 72, Owen, 83, Owen, 88)

In the first FA Cup Final to be held outside of England, and the first to see both sides led by managers from outside of the British Isles, Michael Owen's late double overcame league runners-up Arsenal to seal Liverpool's first FA Cup for nine years.

UEFA Cup Final Westfalenstadion, Dortmund

16/05/2001 / Liverpool vs Alaves

Liverpool /
Westerveld, Babbel, Carragher, Hyypia, Henchoz, McAllister, Murphy, Hamann, Gerrard, Heskey, Owen.
Subs / Arphexad, Vignal, Wright, Barmby, Smicer (Henchoz, 55), Berger (Owen, 78), Fowler (Heskey, 64).

Alaves /
Herrera, Contra, Geli, Karmona, Tellez, Eggen, Cruyff, Astudillo, Tomic, Desio, Moreno.
Subs / Kike, Begona, Ganan, Azkoitia, Alonso (Eggen, 22), Magno (Astudillo, 46), Pablo (Moreno, 64).

Liverpool 5-4 Alaves
(Babbel, 3, Gerrard, 16, Alonso, 26, McAllister, 40, Moreno, 47, Moreno, 49, Fowler, 72, Cruyff, 88, Geli o.g. 116)

Coming into the game with two trophies already in the bag, Gerard Houllier's Liverpool had the opportunity to seal an unprecedented treble against unfancied Spanish side Deportivo Alaves. A nine goal thriller ensued, with Liverpool sealing the victory with an extra time golden own goal as Alaves right back Delfi Geli headed the ball into his own net. Gary McAllister claimed the Man of the Match award in a bad tempered affair which saw Alaves end the game with only 9 men left on the field.

MANAGERS

Rafa Benitez
2004-2010

Taking over from Gerard Houllier, Rafa Benitez will always be remembered by Liverpool fans for masterminding that most remarkable night in Istanbul. He was to spend 6 years at Anfield, adding an FA Cup in 2006 to the 2005 Champions League triumph, and taking Liverpool to second in the Premier League in 2009. Changes in ownership led to boardroom conflicts, and a crisis on the pitch which culminated in the club's worst run since 1987 saw Benitez depart the club by mutual consent in the summer of 2010. During his tenure he got frustratingly close to winning Liverpool's first title of the Premier League era, but ultimately fell short, the early promise of that most glorious of nights sadly unfulfilled.

UEFA Champions League Final
Ataturk Olympic Stadium, Istanbul

25/05/2005 / AC Milan vs Liverpool

AC Milan /
Dida, Cafu, Stam, Nesta, Maldini, Pirlo, Gattuso, Seedorf, Kaka, Shevchenko, Crespo.
Subs / Abbiati, Kaladze, Costacurta, Rui Costa (Gattuso, 112), Dhorasoo, Serginho (Seedorf, 86), Tomasson (Crespo, 85).

Liverpool /
Dudek, Finnan, Carragher, Hyypia, Traore, Alonso, Garcia, Gerrard, Riise, Kewell, Baros.
Subs / Carson, Josemi, Hamann (Finnan, 46), Nunez, Biscan, Cisse (Baros, 85), Smicer (Kewell, 23)

AC Milan 3-3 Liverpool
(Maldini, 1, Crespo, 39, Crespo, 44, Gerrard, 54, Smicer, 56, Alonso, 60). Liverpool win 3-2 on penalties.

Liverpool's remarkable comeback in the 2005 Champions League Final is one of the greatest games in the history of European competition. Despite going three goals behind in the first half to a much fancied Milan side, Liverpool fought back after the break, scoring three times in little more than five minutes to bring the sides level, and force the game to extra time and a 3-2 victory on penalties, as the European Cup returned to Anfield for a fifth time.

FA Cup Final Millennium Stadium, Cardiff

13/05/2006 / Liverpool vs West Ham United

Liverpool /
Reina, Finnan, Riise, Carragher, Hyypia, Gerrard, Kewell, Alonso, Sissoko, Cisse, Crouch.
Subs / Dudek, Kromkamp (Alonso, 67), Traore, Hamann (Crouch, 71), Morientes (Kewell, 48).

West Ham United /
Hislop, Scaloni, Konchesky, Ferdinand, Gabbidon, Benayoun, Etherington, Fletcher, Reo-Coker, Ashton, Harewood.
Subs / Walker, Dailly (Fletcher, 77), Collins, Sheringham (Etherington, 85), Zamora (Ashton, 71).

Liverpool 3-3 West Ham United
(Carragher o.g. 21, Ashton, 28, Cisse, 32, Gerrard, 54, Konchesky, 63, Gerrard, 90+1). Liverpool win 3-1 on penalties.

In the last final to be played in Cardiff before the opening of the new Wembley Stadium, Liverpool twice came from behind to deny West Ham a first FA Cup win since their victory over Arsenal in 1980. Steven Gerrard had already set up Djibril Cisse's 32nd minute goal to get Liverpool back into the tie, as well as rifling home an equaliser on 54, but it is for his 30 yard injury time screamer that the game will be remembered.

Vital Statistics

Most league goals scored in a season	106 in 30 games, 1895-96 (Second Division)
Fewest league goals scored in a season	42 in 34 games, 1901-02, 42 in 42 games, 1970-71 (First Division)
Most league goals conceded in a season	97 in 42 games, 1953-54 (First Division)
Fewest league goals conceded in a season	16 in 42 games, 1978-79 (First Division)
Most points in a season (two points for a win)	68 in 42 games, 1978-79 (First Division)
Most points in a season (three points for a win)	90 in 42 games, 1987-88 (First Division)
Fewest points in a season (two points for a win)	22 in 30 games, 1894-95, (First Division)
Fewest points in a season (three points for a win)	52 points in 38 games, 2011-12 (Premier League)
Record league win	10-1 vs Rotherham Town (February 18, 1896)
Record league defeat	12-1 vs Reading (December 11, 1954)